The Metabolism Diet Cookbook

For Reset Your Metabolism

Kevin D. Jackson

Contents

having to deal with food cravings? Do you too experience fatigue and sluggishness from time to time?

This book is for you if you responded "yes" to one or more of these questions.

I'll describe how our metabolism works, the many kinds of metabolism, and which foods are true metabolism boosters in the first section of this book.

There are various benefits to having a "excellent" metabolism.

In Part II, you'll get step-by-step instructions for growing muscle, as well as helpful hints. Because muscles help you lose weight by supporting an active metabolism and increasing your daily calorie need! Learn which health factors to consider while growing muscle, as well as which diet is best for strength athletes.

You'll be sure to attain your goal weight using my target accomplishment technique in the third section of this book! This strategy, by the way, may be used to achieve any other objective in life.

I also go through proper training (Part IV) and explain what is vital when it comes to gaining muscle growth in an easy-to-understand manner. There are beginner and expert training regimens available, so you can have your ideal physique quickly!

The fifth section of this book contains detailed, practical directions for the hCG / METABOLISM DIET, including numerous recommendations and appropriate dishes. Each of the 21 days of your metabolic diet will include a delectable breakfast, a delectable lunch, and a light supper. Of course, all of the meals are appropriate for a metabolic diet.

More metabolic recipes await you in the sixth section of my guide, so you may add even more diversity to your kitchen!

Nutritional information is included in each of my 124 recipes.

PART I: Introduction to Metabolism

cress butter whole wheat bread pieces

Breakfast: smoked soup with salmon and celery

Ingredients for 1 serving:

30g smoked salmon 20g onion\s150g celeriac\s50ml cooking cream, 7 percent fat 250ml vegetable stock

1 teaspoon butter\steaspoon lemon juice 3g dill\ssalt and pepper

Preparation:\sStep 1: Peel and dice the celeriac. Then sweat the celery cubes with a little butter in a pan and then pour the broth over them. Let everything simmer for about fifteen minutes. Then puree the soup using a hand blender and add the lemon juice. Finally, pour in the cooking cream and season everything to your taste.

Step 2: Chop the dill and cut the fish into strips, sprinkle over the soup.

Medium degree of difficulty Time to prepare: 30 minutes

Lunch: blueberries with curd cheese in a baking dish
Ingredients for 3 servings:

eggs

200ml milk (low fat) (low fat) 500g quark

Blueberries (100g) Sweetener 3 tbsp\spack of sugar-free pudding powder some lemon zest

Preparation:\sStep 1: Heat the oven to 150 ° C. Then stir the eggs with the sweetener in a bowl until frothy. Then stir together the milk, the pudding powder and the quark. Stir in the zest of one lemon.

Step 2: Wash the blueberries, drain them and stir in as well. Put the batter in the baking dish and bake in the oven for 60 minutes.

Total calories: 290 kcal Medium degree of difficulty
Preparation time: 70 minutes

Dinner: Veggie cabbage rolls Ingredients for 4 servings:

¼ white cabbage 1 pepper, yellow 40g quinoa\stomatoes

clove of garlic a single onion

10g butter

Salt, pepper, curry, turmeric and black salt

Preparation:\sStep 1: Remove the leaves from the cabbage
and wash carefully. Then bring salted water to a boil in a
saucepan and add the cabbage leaves. Blanch the cabbage
for around 3 minutes. Soak 40g quinoa in hot salted water
for about 10 minutes.

Step 2: Dice the peppers and the two tomatoes. Then sauté
the garlic and onion in a pan and add the quinoa. Mix
everything and season.

Step 3: Drain the blanched cabbage leaves using a sieve, then
process them into roulades. At the end, put the filling on the
cabbage leaves and fold into parcels. Fix with a toothpick.

Step 4: Finally, let the cabbage rolls melt briefly on both sides in a pan.

Total calories: 101 kcal

Medium degree of difficulty Preparation time: 25 minutes

Day 16

Breakfast : spinach omelette

Ingredients:\smedium sized eggs 1 onion (small)

1 handful of spinach leaves 3 cherry tomatoes

dash of milk (low-fat) (low-fat) seasonings

Preparation:\sStep 1: Finely cut the kitchen onions & sauté them briefly.

Wash the spinach, spin dry and add to the onion in the pan. Fry everything properly.

Step 2: Wash the cherry tomatoes, cut in half and add to the pan. Then beat the eggs and whisk them with a dash of milk. Season with salt and pepper to your taste.

Total calories: 192 kcal Medium apprehension level 15 minutes for preparation

Lunch: Mint-Feta-Melon Salad Ingredients:

180g light feta cheese 800g watermelon pulp Mint leaves (handful) colored pepper

Preparation:\sStep 1: Cut the feta and watermelon into small cubes.

At the same time, wash off the mint leaves and mix everything together in a bowl. Season to taste with pepper - preferably freshly ground.

Total calories: 221 kcal Easy level of difficulty Preparation time: 5-10 minutes

Dinner: protein crepes Ingredients:\s120ml unsweetened almond milk 10g coconut flour

10g protein powder whey 6g flaxseed

3g psyllium husks 1 egg

Preparation:\sStep 1: Mix all ingredients and let thicken. Then bake the protein crêpes very thinly in a coated pan.

Total calories: 176 kcal Easy level of difficulty 15 minutes for preparation

Day 17

Breakfast: low carb egg muffins

Ingredients:\smedium sized eggs 25g lean ham cubes 1 medium onion

30g grated cheese 3 cocktail tomatoes salt pepper

Preparation:\sStep 1: Preheat the oven to 180°C, prepare a 6-cup muffin pan and put on the muffin tins. Step 2: Wash and quarter the tomatoes, also dice the peeled onion. Whisk the eggs with the other ingredients well and season.

Step 3: Fill the mold with egg mixture and bake for a quarter of an hour.

Total calories: 297 kcal Level of difficulty: simple Preparation time: 25 minutes

Lunch: pizza with tuna bottom Ingredients:\s1 can of tuna (natural) (natural) 2 eggs\shalf can of chunky tomatoes 1 large mushroom\sclove of garlic

50g grated cheese (lean level) (lean level) 3 tbsp pizza seasoning Optional: basil leaves

Preparation:

Step 1: Preheat your oven to 220 °C convection and let the tuna drain well. Then mix the whole tuna with the eggs.

Step 2: Spread the tuna and egg mixture in a circle on a baking sheet and bake in the oven until golden brown. At the same time, cut the mushroom into slices and chop the clove of garlic into small pieces. Mix the pizza seasoning together with the chunky tomatoes and garlic.

Step 3: Spread the homemade tomato sauce on the pizza base, sprinkle cheese over it and put the mushroom slices on top. Finally bake for a few minutes.

Total calories: 255 kcal Level of difficulty: simple Preparation time: 25 minutes

Dinner: low carb chips, homemade Ingredients:

50g cheese (light) (light) Raw ham

Paprika spice, pepper

Preparation:\sStep 1: Dice the raw ham with a knife & mix with the cheese.

Cut the baking paper to the size of a plate. Make small piles of the ham and cheese on the baking paper. Keep enough distance so that the piles do not mix with one another.

Step 2: Season & microwave for 2 min at 700 watts.

The chips have to be light brown, if they are not,then always for another 20 seconds.

Total calories: 134 kcal Level of difficulty: simple Time to prepare: ten minutes

Day 18

Protein-nut mix for breakfast

Ingredients:

50g whey protein powder 100 mL low-fat milk 2 eggs

80 grams of peanut butter

30 g combination of nut kernels 50g almond flour, sweetener (de-oiled)

Step 1: Preheat the oven to 175 degrees Celsius (convection). Combine the eggs, protein powder, 100ml milk, and the other ingredients in a mixing bowl until a batter is formed. The dough should then be spread out on a baking sheet coated with parchment paper.

Step 2: Preheat the oven to 175°C and bake everything for 10 minutes.

Calories in total: 157 kcal Level of difficulty: easy Time to prepare: 20 minutes

Lunch is prepared at home. 300g canned sauerkraut (carbohydrates to be aware of) Ham is a kind of meat that is (lean stage)

Step 1: Chop or quarter the cooked ham and combine it with the sauerkraut in a microwave-safe bowl.

Calories in total: 111 kcal

Level of difficulty: easy Time to prepare: 2–5 minutes

Cheese and turkey meatballs for dinner Ingredients:

Quark (low-fat) 100g 100g turkey mince a single egg

50 g cheese, grated (lean level) a single garlic clove

1 tablespoon curry powder

1 teaspoon powdered paprika salt and pepper half an onion

Step 1: Prepare a baking sheet and preheat the oven to 180 degrees Celsius.

The onion should next be peeled and diced. Then, except for the turkey mince, chop the garlic and combine all of the ingredients.

Step 2: Using your hands, toss the turkey mince into the prepared mixture and combine everything. Then, using your hands, form the mixture into tiny meatballs.

Step 3: Bake the meatballs for about a quarter hour.

Calories in total: 375 kcal Medium degree of difficulty Time to prepare: 30 minutes

Day 19

Breakfast: shellfish salad with rocket

150g king prawns (about) 150 grams of rocket salad a single onion

1 vine tomato, half a pepper, a drizzle of balsamic vinegar, and a pinch of salt and pepper

Step 1: Fry the king prawns in a greased pan for a few seconds on each sides. The bell pepper, vine tomato, and onion are then diced. Remove the prawns from the pan after they've been seared for a few minutes and cook the veggies in the leftover liquid.

Step 2: Drizzle balsamic vinegar, olive oil, and spices over the salad. Finally, combine all of the ingredients and place on a dish.

Calories in total: 187 kcal Medium degree of difficulty Time to prepare: 15 minutes

Crispy Garlic Chicken for Lunch Ingredients:

3 g of garlic 30 mL extra virgin olive oil

10 g parmesan cheese, grated 15 g breadcrumbs, dry

chicken breast halves, 100g Preparation: Preheat the oven to 220 degrees Celsius. Then, in a bowl, combine the parmesan and breadcrumbs and sauté the garlic and onion well.

Step 2: Place the chicken, garlic cloves, and oil in a pot and flip it over. The chicken is then breaded with breadcrumbs and parmesan cheese.

Step 3: Place the chicken in a good shape and bake for 30 to 35 minutes in the oven.

Calories in total: 229 kcal Level of difficulty: easy Time to prepare: 45 minutes stuffed mushrooms for dinner

50g chunky tomatoes (optional) 6 mushrooms 100g turkey mince

1 tablespoon of Italian herbs

1 teaspoon meat seasoning, minced

Step 1: Preheat the oven to 220°C with circulating air.

Wash the mushrooms, remove the stem, then use a spoon to gently scrape out the head. Half of the mushroom stems should be diced.

Step 2: Season the minced turkey with salt and pepper, then combine with the herbs and mushroom stems. Fill the mushroom caps with the mixed turkey mince and a teaspoon of chunky tomatoes.

Step 3: Bake the filled mushrooms for 20 to 25 minutes in the oven.

Calories in total: 227 kcal Medium degree of difficulty Time to prepare: 35 minutes

Breakfast: cucumber roller with protein

20th day

1 serving's ingredients are as follows:

1 slice of cucumber Salmon (80g)

cream cheese, 20 g

a tablespoon of soy sauce

1 tablespoon of marine algae (available in well-stocked drugstores or on the Internet)

Step 1: Remove the cucumber stem from the cucumber and wash it under cold water. Cut cucumber strips with a vegetable peeler; for the salmon, cut around 8-10 strips. Place the salmon strips on kitchen paper and cover them with a kitchen towel to absorb any remaining moisture. The fish should then be chopped into tiny pieces and placed in a kitchen basin.

Step 2: In a mixing dish, combine the seaweed, cream cheese, and soy sauce and stir until the cream cheese is evenly spread beneath the salmon.

Step 3: On the end of a cucumber strip, insert a teaspoon of salmon 2cm long. From this side, roll up the salmon. Finally, use a toothpick to secure everything in place. Use the whole contents of the dish to consume all of the rolls.

Calories in total: 215 kcal Medium degree of difficulty Time to prepare: 10 minutes

Lunch consists of veggie fries.

a single egg

3 medium-sized mushrooms 100 g peppers, mixed a half onion

1 tomato, big Parsely

coconut oil, 5 mL salt & pepper with dill

Step 1: Clean and dice tomatoes, mushrooms, peppers, and onions. In a mixing bowl, season everything and stir in the dill and parsley. In a nonstick pan, fry the contents of the bowl with the coconut oil.

Step 2: In a separate dish, beat or combine the eggs with the seasonings.

Reduce the heat to low and pour the final egg mixture into the pan, allowing it to set. At the end, cut and divide.

Calories in total: 195 kcal Medium degree of difficulty Time to prepare: 25 minutes

Dinner: tomato-eggs in the oven

100 g tomatoes, chunky 1 egg, medium size a half onion

1 teaspoon pesto verde 25 g parmesan cheese, grated 5 leaves of basil

1 teaspoon extra virgin olive oil

1 teaspoon oregano, dry salt with pepper

Preparation: Step 1: Preheat the oven and peel the onion in the meanwhile. Then dice them finely and sauté them in a little amount of olive oil. Season everything to taste with the chunky tomatoes in the pan. The basil should then be chopped and added.

Step 2: Toss the pesto and eggs into the sauce in the pan, then top with parmesan. Finally, bake everything for about 15 minutes in the oven.

Calories in total: 263 kcal

Level of difficulty: easy Time to prepare: 30 minutes

21st day

Chia pudding for breakfast

1 serving's ingredients are as follows:

chia seeds, 5 tbsp 150 milliliters almond milk berries in season

Step 1: Place the chia seeds in a small bowl, cover with almond milk, and let aside for 15 minutes. Step 2: Stir in fresh berries as desired after the seeds are puffed and have a pudding-like consistency.

Calories in total: 174 kcal Level of difficulty: easy Time to prepare: 20 minutes

Soup with vegetables for lunch 1 serving's ingredients are as follows:

Carrots, 100g medium potato 100g broccoli Milk, 150 mL (low fat) nutmeg, salt, and pepper

Step 1: Cook the peeled and diced veggies for a quarter of an hour in a little water until tender.

Step 2: Using a hand blender, purée the soup after pouring the milk over the veggies. Season to taste and pour over the soup as desired.

Calories in total: 178 kcal Level of difficulty: easy Time to prepare: 25 minutes

Dinner: cress on whole wheat bread 1 serving's ingredients are as follows:

Step 1: Spread a thin layer of butter on the bread and top with fresh cress.

1 serving nutritional values:

41.4 g carbohydrate, 7.2 g protein

6.30g fat

Calories in total: 252 kcal Level of difficulty: easy Time to prepare: 5 minutes

PART VI: 61 metabolic recipes

Chapter 3

Chicken with red cabbage and mustard

Breakfast

Yogurt in a frozen form with a lemon and mint sauce

Ingredients:

1 lemon (1 slice) 200 grams of yogurt (low fat)

gelatin sheets (three pieces) 1 teaspoon stevia extract

10 mint leaves 1 tablespoon erythritol

Step 1: Finely cut the mint, then combine it with the lemon in a blender with the stevia and purée until smooth. Step 2: Make gelatine by dissolving it in boiling water and then squeezing it out. Combine the gelatin mass, yogurt, and lemon sauce in a mixing bowl. Then relax.

Calories in total: 388 kcal Medium degree of difficulty Time to prepare: 60 minutes

Tortilla chunks that are crunchy

6 servings of ingredients:

4 tacos de tortilla 2 tbsp extra virgin olive oil a single lime

2 jalapeos, tiny

1 tbsp tequila 1 teaspoon honey 2 spring onions 450g tuna fillet 150g avocado sesame seeds tablespoons

12 tsp cumin powder

Step 1: Using a cutter, cut 4 circles out of the tortilla, coat each side with oil, and salt one side each. Bake for 8-10 minutes, salt side up, at 175 degrees. Chop the jalapeos and squeeze the lime.

Step 2: In a bowl, combine the cumin, lime juice, tequila, and honey, along with salt and pepper. Toss the tuna with a little oil and dice it. Spring onions should be chopped into tiny bits. The avocado should be peeled and the pulp diced.

Step 3: Toss the tuna, onions, and avocado with the marinade, then serve on tortillas with sesame seeds sprinkled on top.

Calories in total: 190 kcal Medium degree of difficulty Time to prepare: 30 minutes

Figs and Parma ham

4 servings of ingredients:

4 figs 8 parma ham

tbsp olive oil 2 mint stalks 12 lemon teaspoon liquid honey black mill pepper (cold pressed)

Step 1: Season the Parma ham generously with salt and pepper, then cut the figs in half and arrange them on top of the ham. Mint leaves should be washed and carefully chopped, and the lemon should be squeezed. Drizzle the lemon juice, honey, and olive oil over the figs.

Calories in total: 156 kcal Level of difficulty: easy Time to prepare: 15 minutes

On seaweed, pesto and tomatoes

Ingredients:

50g pasta with algae (available in well-stocked drugstores, pharmacies or on the Internet) 30 grams of pine nuts

cherry tomatoes (200g) 2 tablespoons extra virgin olive oil basil (two stalks)

2 tbsp pesto verde

1 tsp. agave nectar salt with pepper

Step 1: Soak the seaweed pasta in a basin of tepid water for 20 minutes before cooking in boiling water with a pinch of salt for another 20 minutes.

In a skillet, toast the pine nuts until golden brown, then heat the oil, braise the tomatoes, and season.

Drizzle agave syrup on top.

Step 2: Drain the algae paste and add it to the tomato pan, along with the pesto and seasonings. Serve with pine nuts and basil.

Calories in total: 220 kcal Medium degree of difficulty Time to prepare: 60 minutes

3 eggs 3 eggs 3 eggs 3 eggs 3 eggs 3 eggs 3 eggs 3 eggs 3 eggs 3 eggs 3 eggs 3

a single tomato

nutmeg, salt, and pepper parsley (fresh)

Step 1: In a small kitchen basin, mix together the eggs using a fork.

Then add the diced tomato pieces and parsley and mix well.

Step 2: Whisk the egg in a hot pan until it begins to solidify.

Calories in total: 240 kcal Level of difficulty: easy Time to prepare: 10 minutes

Muesli with blueberries

Ingredients:

1 handful of blueberries, fresh 50g oats + a handful of chopped nuts 150 milliliters almond milk

Step 1: Pour the almond milk over the oat flakes and infuse for 2 minutes before topping with blueberries and almonds.

Calories in total: 317 kcal Level of difficulty: easy Time to prepare: 5 minutes meat-based main meals

Noodles made from zucchini ribbons with minced pork and a coconut sauce

Ingredients:

120g lean beef mince a sprinkle of curry powder 200ml coconut milk 1 tsp. pepper, chopped zucchini

Step 1: Lightly sauté the mince, then pour in the coconut milk, season with paprika and curry powder, pepper, and simmer. Blanch the zucchinis for 4 minutes after peeling and cutting them into thin strips.

Step 2: Arrange the zucchini on a platter and drizzle with the sauce.

Calories in total: 337 kcal Medium degree of difficulty Time to prepare: 40 minutes

Peas with ham-based carbonara

Ingredients for a four-person meal:

1 garlic onion clove

100g streaky bacon, smoked 30 g parmesan cheese

0.5 tbsp ground almonds (organic lemon) 300g spaghetti (whole wheat) coarse pepper, salt

peas (150g) (frozen) two eggs 200g yogurt (cream)

Preparation: Cut the garlic, onion, and bacon into tiny pieces in the first step.

Grate the parmesan cheese finely. Rub the peel of the lemon after washing it in hot water. In a non-stick pan, roast the almonds while frying the bacon. Add the garlic and onion in a few minutes later.

Step 2: Prepare and cook the spaghetti; add the peas just before the noodles are done. Season the eggs and yoghurt mixture.

Step 3: Drain the pasta, reserving 150ml of the cooking liquid. In a large mixing bowl, combine the peas and pasta, add the pasta water, and whisk together the egg mixture. Serve with a sprinkling of almonds.

Calories in total: 460 kcal Medium degree of difficulty Time to prepare: 30 minutes

Chili with carne made with pumpkin and beets.

4 servings of ingredients:

a single onion (red)

200 g Hokkaido pumpkin 500 g ground beef garlic cloves 30g paste de tomate 200 grams of beets

4 tbsp olive oil

2 tablespoons ajvar

1 teaspoon cayenne pepper

850g tomatoes, chunky (approx. 1 can) 1 teaspoon powdered vegetable stock

1 tablespoon balsamic vinaigrette peppers de chile

salt with pepper

Preparation: Cut the garlic and onion into tiny pieces in the first step. Roughly dice the pumpkin (the peel of the Hokkaido pumpkin may be eaten). Slice the leek into thin rings, reserving a few green ones for decoration. The beetroot should next be peeled and sliced into small pieces.

Step 2: Season the ground beef with chili, pepper, and salt after frying it in a skillet for a few minutes until it's done.

Remove the flesh.

Step 3: Fry the pumpkin, leek, garlic, and onion for 2 minutes in the frying grease. Cook for another 2 minutes after adding the tomato paste. Pour 200 mL of water into the pot, then add the chunky tomatoes. Stir in the ajvar and stock powder, and bring to a boil for a few minutes. Season with salt and pepper after adding the beets and minced meat. Allow the stew to simmer for 25 minutes on low heat.

Step 4: Toss the remaining leek rings on top of the chilli con carne just before serving.

Calories in total: 380 kcal Medium degree of difficulty Time to prepare: 40 minutes

Ingredients:

Chicken breast, 200 g 300 grams of red cabbage

mustard (three teaspoons) curry powder (1 teaspoon) 1 garlic clove tbsp vegetable stock 2 tablespoons apple cider vinegar

Step 1: prepare the vegetable stock and garlic. Combine the red cabbage, vinegar, and pepper in a mixing bowl. After that, cook. Step 2: Cook the chicken in a skillet with the mustard and curry spice.

Calories in total: 192 kcal Medium degree of difficulty Time to prepare: 40 minutes

Burger made with sweet potatoes

Ingredients:

tbsp lime juice 300g sweet potato garlic

1 tbsp agave nectar extra virgin olive oil

a half avocado

1 teaspoon paprika powder (hot) 3 tbsp natural low-fat yogurt

wasabi paste (1 teaspoon) 2 onions, red

400g minced meat (mixed) Paste made from tomatoes

50 g mixed lettuce

Step 1: Preheat your oven to roughly 200 degrees Celsius. Then cut the sweet potatoes into slices and combine them with the fiery paprika powder and olive oil in a mixing dish. After that, bake the potato slices for 20-25 minutes in the oven.

Step 2: Peel and finely cut the garlic. Remove the stone from the avocado and gently scoop out the flesh with a spoon. Combine the natural yoghurt, 2 tablespoons water, lime juice, wasabi paste, garlic, and agave syrup in a mixing bowl.

Everything should be pureed using a hand blender and seasoned to taste.

Step 3: Chop the kitchen onion finely and combine it with the minced beef, mustard, and tomato paste in a mixing bowl. Season this mixture with a lot of pepper and salt. Form the mince into patties and cook them for 6-8 minutes on medium heat.

Step 4: Remove the sweet potato slices from the oven and season with salt. 1 additional onion, as well as tomatoes, should be cut into slices. Toss the salad in a circle. Patties, tomatoes, onion rings, lettuce, wasabi-avocado sauce, and lastly another sweet potato slice go on top of the sweet potato slice.

Calories in total: 380 kcal Level of difficulty: tough Time to prepare: 60 minutes

Zucchini lasagna with minced zucchini

Ingredients:

150 g mozzarella cheese

75 grams of crème fraîche (low fat) 2 zucchini, minced (400g) 400 grams of tomatoes

Step 1: Peel the zucchini and cut it into slices before preheating the oven. In the gratin dish, layer the tomato slices as a basis and then distribute the minced beef on top. Finally, drizzle with crème fraîche and top with a second layer of tomato.

Step 2: Finally, sprinkle a layer of mozzarella on top. Preheat oven to 350°F and bake for 30 minutes.

Calories in total: 533 kcal Medium degree of difficulty Time to prepare: 60 minutes

Chapter 4

Vegetable pizza pan

Legs of chicken

Ingredients:

3 vine tomatoes 1 piece of chicken thigh

zucchini (1 piece)

1 teaspoon Provence herb 1 tablespoon extra virgin olive oil

Step 1: Preheat the oven to 180°C and massage the sambal oelek and garlic into the chicken, then sprinkle with paprika powder.

Allow to finish cooking in the oven pan. The vine tomatoes and zucchini should then be cut into slices and placed in an ovenproof baking tray.

Step 2: pour in the water, season the legs with herbs, and add the veggies. Preheat oven to 150°C and bake for around 25 minutes.

Calories in total: 406 kcal Medium degree of difficulty Time to prepare: 60 minutes

Beef and broccoli stir-fry with sesame nuts

Ingredients:

1 tablespoon of coconut oil 10g sesame seeds 400g beef fillet

1 tblsp sesame seed oil 500g broccoli 1 sprinkle of salt 1 onion, green

3 garlic cloves 1 teaspoon of ginger 1 cayenne pepper

Step 1: Cut the beef fillet into slices and bring a pot of water to a boil. Rinse the broccoli florets in cold water after 5 minutes in the water. The onion, ginger, and garlic should all be peeled, and the chilli pepper should be cored and diced.

Step 2: In a skillet, fry the vegetable onion, then add the meat, broccoli, and cover to simmer. Sesame seeds should be sprinkled over everything.

Calories in total: 532 kcal Medium degree of difficulty Time to prepare: 30 minutes

Chicken breast calzone

Ingredients:

Chicken breast, 200 g a single eggplant

1 courgette

1 pepper (bell)

a single onion

1 tomato sauce can with garlic, chopped into bits 50 g cheese, grated (light)

oregano, rosemary

Step 1: Prepare the veggies and onion by washing, peeling, and dicing them.

After that, combine everything in a gratin dish. Season with a teaspoon of salt and pepper and pour the tomato sauce over the veggies.

Step 2: Cook the veggies in the gratin dish in the oven for approximately a quarter of an hour at 180°C.

In a skillet, fry the beef until it is slightly pink in the centre.

Cut lengthwise, season with salt and pepper, then stuff with cheese and tomato sauce.

Place the meat in the gratin dish, then sprinkle the cheese over the top.

Step 3: Return the casserole to the oven for 15 minutes more.

Calories in total: 332 kcal Medium degree of difficulty Time to prepare: 30 minutes

Stew from Pichelsteiner

6 servings of ingredients:

Waxy potatoes, 400g 4 garlic cloves, big onions Carrots, 100g savoy cabbage, 500g 150 grams of beef goulash

200 grams of lean meat (e.g. turkey)

200 g of pork season with salt and pepper

stalks of marjoram, rosemary, and thyme tbsp rapeseed oil 700ml vegetable stock

Step 1: Crush the garlic cloves. Finely chop the onion, carrots, savoy cabbage, and potatoes. Season all kinds of meat thoroughly before cutting into bite-sized chunks. Preheat the oven to 160 degrees Celsius after picking the rosemary, marjoram, and thyme (convection).

Step 2: Sear the meat all over and remove 2/3 of it from the saucepan. Season half of the veggies in a pot.

Step 3: Return the other meat to the pot and cover it with the remaining veggies. Pour in the broth, season with salt and pepper, and bring to a boil. Cook for 90 minutes after that.

Calories in total: 250 kcal Medium degree of difficulty Time to prepare: 30 minutes

Ingredients: onions (spring)

1 carrot, 1 zucchini pepper, 1 carrot, 1 zucchini pepper, 1 zucchini pepper, 1

rapeseed oil, 2 tablespoons 1 tsp oregano (oregano)

tomato strains, 2 tbsp

100g chicken slices (low-fat) 1 tablespoon mozzarella cheese (grated) black mill pepper, salt

Step 1: First, slice the spring onion into fine rolls.

The zucchini and carrots should next be peeled and sliced into slices. The bell peppers should then be washed and sliced into bite-sized pieces. In a greased pan, heat a little rapeseed oil. Add the veggies, oregano, and 2 tablespoons of water to the pan and cook for a few minutes. Then add the tomatoes to deglaze the pan. After that, remove the pan from the heat and season everything to your liking.

Step 2: Chop the chicken into tiny pieces and toss it in with the veggies. Allow to cool. Place the dish on plates and top with mozzarella cheese.

Calories in total: 320 kcal Medium degree of difficulty Time to prepare: 30 minutes

Salad with potatoes and lamb

(4 servings) Ingredients:

150g rocket or mixed lettuce 300g lamb fillet Waxy potatoes, 600g

2 peppers (red)

100g mozzarella balls, seasoned with a sprinkle of salt

pepper with curry powder

lemon juice, 2 tbsp 4 tbsp extra virgin olive oil

2 tbsp balsamic vinegar

Step 1: Cut the peppers in quarters and set them skin side up on a baking sheet. Cook for around 10 minutes on the grill. Cut the peppers into strips when they have cooled completely. Then quarter the potatoes and sprinkle with olive oil gently. Preheat the oven to 200°C and bake the wedges for 30 to 35 minutes.

Step 2: Wash the rocket or lettuce mixture and tear the leaves into bite-sized pieces.

The mozzarella should then be drained.

Season the lamb fillet and cook it in a nonstick pan for a few minutes. 10 minutes before the end of the cooking period, place the meat and potatoes in the oven. Brush the roasted potatoes with a mixture of curry powder and a tablespoon of olive oil.

Step 3: Combine the lemon juice, wine vinegar, and the remaining olive oil in a mixing bowl, then add the lettuce and season to taste. On top, scatter mozzarella balls. Place the meat on top.

Calories in total: 376 kcal Level of difficulty: tough Time to prepare: 60 minutes

Veggie omelette with minced meat

2 eggs are required.

30 mL of milk (low fat)

broccoli and cauliflower, 150 g tomato paste, 3 tbsp

200g beef mince

Step 1: Cut the cauliflower or broccoli florets into tiny pieces.

Add the tomato paste to the pan with the rapeseed oil. Combine the milk and the eggs in a mixing bowl.

Step 2: Pour the egg-milk mixture into a hot pan and let it to set. After that, pull it out and wrap it up.

Calories in total: 359 kcal Medium degree of difficulty Time to prepare: 60 minutes

Arabic chicken

Ingredients:

Chicken breast fillet, 100g 1 bunch coriander lime zest onion bits a single garlic clove 1 garlic clove

4 tomatillos

nutmeg, crushed coriander, and a pinch of curry powder

cardamom, salt, and pepper

Step 1: Finely dice the tomatoes and onions in the kitchen.

Season the meat with salt and pepper, then mince the garlic. Then shred the lime peel and chop the coriander into thin pieces.

Step 2: Sear the chicken breasts and cook the garlic and onions in a skillet.

In a pan, combine the clove, nutmeg, coriander spice, cardamom, onions, and lime zest.

Step 3: pour in 300ml of water and the tomatoes, cover, and cook for 15 minutes. Step 4: Add the meat and simmer for another 5 minutes.

Calories in total: 153 kcal Medium degree of difficulty Time to prepare: 45 minutes

Fish-based main meals

Basil pesto with freshwater fish

Ingredients:

800g broccoli 15g pesto 1 chili pepper 400g pikeperch fillet

Step 1: Season the fish with chile and pepper and fry it on both sides. Broccoli should be simmered in a colander over a pot.

Calories in total: 202 kcal Medium degree of difficulty Time to prepare: 60 minutes

Capers and tuna cream baked tomatoes

4 servings of ingredients:

800g tomato, egg two garlic cloves 2 tbsp extra virgin olive oil tuna, 270g

150 gram of yogurt (low fat) sour cream (125g) (low fat)

12 lemons capers (40g)

rosemary, thyme 1 celery stalk

1 salad with fine leaves

Step 1: Cut the tomatoes in half and set aside. In a bowl, finely dice the garlic and combine with the thyme, rosemary, 1 tablespoon olive oil, and salt & pepper. Then pour the sauce over the tomatoes and arrange them cut side down on the grid. Dry tomatoes in the oven for 2-3 hours at 110 degrees.

Step 2: Squeeze the lemon, then blend the drained tuna with the yogurt, sour cream, capers, olive oil, and lemon juice until smooth.

Step 3: Finely chop the celery and tear the lettuce into bite-sized pieces. On top, pour the tomatoes and tuna caper cream.

Total calories: 195 kcal Medium degree of difficulty Time to prepare: 3.5 hours

Zoodles with shrimp, spinach, and tomatoes

Ingredients:

Cocktail tomatoes with coconut oil spinach (6 pieces) 1 tsp lemon extract prawns 200g zucchini

Step 1: Use a spiral cutter to chop the zucchini and sauté the prawns.

In a separate pan, heat the zoodles, tomatoes, and spinach. Combine all of the ingredients.

Calories in total: 257 kcal Medium degree of difficulty Time to prepare: 20 minutes

Ceviche with sweet potatoes and white fish

Ingredients for a four-person meal:

4 sweet potatoes, tiny

oregano, chili flakes (or Mediterranean herb mixture)

a dozen lemons four limes

1 red chili pepper, tiny a single garlic clove

1 piece of ginger the size of a hazelnut 1 onion, red

1 cucumber (organic)

1 peach (firm)

12 coriander bunch

400g fillet of white fish (cod, sea bream)

black pepper, sea salt a little olive oil Preparation:

1st step: Preheat the oven to 180 degrees Celsius, then cut the sweet potatoes in half and season with oregano, chili, pepper, and salt. Drizzle the lemon juice over the potatoes and serve them with the sliced side facing down. Then sprinkle with lemon juice and bake for approximately half an hour with the sliced surface facing down. Allow everything to acquire a lovely golden brown color. Squeeze the lime juice into a mixing bowl.

Step 2: Remove the seeds from the chili pepper, break them up, and toss them into the mixing bowl. Season with salt after squeezing the garlic and ginger into the lime juice. The onion should now be sliced into tiny rings. Cucumbers should be quartered and cored. Remove the stone from the peach, peel it, and quarter it. Remove the coriander leaves with your fingers. Cut the fish into bite-size pieces, then add it to the lime mixture and simmer for 5 minutes before adding the rest of the ingredients. Combine all of the ingredients and drain any remaining lime juice. Season the ceviche with salt.

calorie total: 300 kcal Medium degree of difficulty Time to prepare: 45 minutes

Salmon and veggies in a tin

4 oz. frozen salmon fillets 400 oz. potatoes

2 onions (spring)

200g physalis zucchini 1 fennel bulb

thyme, thyme, rosemary, rosemary, rosemary, rosemary, rosemary, rosemary, rosemary, rosemary, rosemary, rosemary a little olive oil

Step 1: Slice the potatoes and zucchini, dice the fennel, slice the onions into rings, and remove the fruit from the shell.

Step 2: Brush the baking sheet with olive oil, arrange the salmon fillets in the center, and cover with veggies and potatoes. Season with pepper and salt to taste, then garnish with the herbs.

Step 3: Preheat oven to 180°C and bake for 35 minutes. 8 minutes before the finish, drizzle with fruit.

1 serving nutritional values:

Calories in total: 275 kcal Medium degree of difficulty Time to prepare: 20 minutes

rosso and sprouted smoked fish

Ingredients:

12 bunch of radishes 1 head of Lollo Rosso or oak leaf

organic cucumber, tiny 1 tablespoon tahini (sesame paste) 1 garlic clove, sliced pumpernickel 12 lemons tbsp olive oil 2 smoked char fillets handful of purple radish sprouts salt and pepper

Cleaning, washing, and plucking the lettuce are the first steps in the preparation process. Then cut the radishes into thin slices. Dice half of the cucumber, put the sesame paste, 1 tablespoon olive oil, lemon juice, garlic and spices in a bowl and puree. Slice the other half of the cucumber.

Step 2: Dice and fry the pumpernickel, cut the char into bite-sized pieces. Put the salad ingredients in two bowls, pour over the dressing. Give everything over the char fillets.

Total calories: 360 kcal Medium degree of difficulty Time to prepare: 20 minutes

Beetroot with saithe

Ingredients:\s400g saithe 500g beetroot 15g coconut oil 1 egg\s30g almond flour Basil leaves

Preparation:\sStep 1: Mix the egg in a bowl, brush the fish with the egg and turn in almond flour. Then fry the fish until golden

Step 2: Cut the beetroot into slices, serve on a plate with the fish and basil.

Total calories: 442 kcal Medium degree of difficulty Time to prepare: 30 minutes

Marinated tuna

Ingredients:\s150g tuna steak 30g capers

100g cherry tomatoes 1 onion, red

1 cayenne pepper

1 tablespoon balsamic vinaigrette 1 stalk of oregano

season with salt and pepper

Preparation:\sStep 1: Chop the chilli pepper, mix with paprika powder.

Turn the tuna over, let it steep.

Step 2: Finely dice the onions, chop the tomatoes, coarsely chop the capers. Then mix in a bowl with vinegar, season. Peel oregano leaves, roughly chop and add to the bowl.

Total calories: 233 kcal Level of difficulty: easy Time to prepare: 30 minutes

Salmon roll with spinach

Ingredients:

250g smoked salmon 200g cream cheese 75g grated cheese

4 eggs

230g spinach

Preparation:\sStep 1: Preheat oven to 200 °C convection. Beat eggs until frothy, stir in cheese and spinach, season. Bake everything for ten minutes. Mix the cream cheese and lemon and roll up with the salmon.

Total calories: 616 kcal Level of difficulty: easy Time to prepare: 30 minutes

Espresso lentils with prawns

Ingredients for a four-person meal:

50ml white wine 50ml espresso 150g beluga lentils 1 stick of cinnamon 1 bay leaf

1 chilli pepper (dried) (dried) 1 carrot\s½ stick of leek Milk, 150 mL (low fat) 150g cocktail tomatoes

12 large prawns (ready to cook) (ready to cook)

Sea salt, pepper, a little balsamic vinegar Rapeseed oil, olive oil

Preparation:

Step 1: Simmer the lentils with spices in boiling water for about 15 minutes and drain. Peel the carrot, finely dice the leek, sauté in the rapeseed oil. Deglaze with espresso and milk. Simmer for 3 minutes, add the lentils, mix them with the vinegar and salt.

Step 2: Fry the prawns in a pan for 3-5 minutes, season.

Then fry the tomatoes alone in the same pan. Sprinkle with sea salt and deglaze with wine.

Total calories: 140 kcal Medium degree of difficulty Time to prepare: 40 minutes

Trout with radish and cucumber

Ingredients:

Chapter 5

Baked cauliflower curry style

\stbsp soy sauce\steaspoons of lemon juice

Preparation;\sStep 1: Mix the lemon juice, soy sauce and sweetener. Slice the cucumber, also the radish. Put the fish in the marinade & arrange on a plate with cucumber & radish.

Total calories: 127 kcal

Level of difficulty: easy

Time to prepare: 15 minutes

Main courses vegetarian

Almond cream cheese soup

Ingredients:\shalf a lemon

200g cream cheese a single garlic clove

4 tablespoons of flaked almonds 400g broccoli

500ml vegetable stock basil

Preparation:\sStep 1: Cut the broccoli into fine florets and then finely chop the garlic. Simmer the garlic and broccoli in the vegetable stock. Roast the almonds without oil, wash the lemon with hot water.

Step 2: Add the cream cheese / basil leaves and puree.

Total calories: 307 kcal Level of difficulty: easy Time to prepare: 30 minutes

Whole grain pasta salad

Ingredients for 8 people:

2 nectarines

6 tbsp olive oil

2 teaspoons of honey

500g whole wheat pasta (e.g. fusilli) Half a bunch of parsley

50g green olives without stones 100g blue cheese

50g almonds

4 cloves of garlic Pepper salt,\s1 red chilli pepper

Preparation:\sStep 1: Cut the nectarines into thin wedges and fry them in a tablespoon of olive oil for 3-4 minutes. Brush with honey, salt and pepper.

Step 2: Let the whole wheat pasta cook in water. Pluck the parsley and finely chop the garlic and chilli pepper. Then put half of the parsley aside and finely chop the rest.

Step 3: Drain the pasta using a sieve. Now fry the chopped parsley, garlic and chilli briefly in a pan and toss the pasta in them.

Step 3: Roughly chop the olives and almonds. Divide the blue cheese. Fold the nectarines, almonds, olives, cheese and the rest of the parsley into the pasta. Finally, pepper and salt as you like.

Total calories: 432 kcal Medium degree of difficulty Time to prepare: 40 minutes

Avocado with tomato salsa

4 servings of ingredients:

green chilli pepper 1 blue onion

1 lemon

6 tomatoes\savocados

wheat tortilla cakes season with salt and pepper

3 tbsp oil

Preparation:\sStep 1: Core the chilli pepper, remove the inner skins, chop finely. Dice the onion, scald tomatoes, halve, core and dice. Mix in the same way, squeeze the lemon, add the juice, mix in the oil and season with pepper.

Step 2: Stone and halve the avocado, drizzle with a little lemon juice. Heat wheat tortilla cakes (oven, pan) and sprinkle with avocado and tomato salsa.

Total calories: 385 kcal Level of difficulty: easy Time to prepare: 15 minutes

Pasta with a pumpkin and sage sauce

4 servings of ingredients:

350g wholemeal ribbon noodles two garlic cloves

600g pumpkin pulp 100ml vegetable stock 2 sprigs of thyme

2 stalks of sage 1 organic lemon

Pepper, salt, olive oil

Preparation:\sStep 1: Cook the pasta in boiling salted water for a few minutes and cut the garlic into fine slices. Cut the pumpkin pulp thinly into slices. Fry the pumpkin slices & garlic until golden brown. Rub 1 teaspoon of lemon zest, squeeze out the juice and add the stock to the pumpkin, let simmer for 5 minutes over a medium heat.

Step 2: Pluck the leaves from the thyme and sage, then mix with the lemon zest and vegetables and season. Drain the pasta, add to the vegetables, mix and season again with the spices.

Total calories: 378 kcal Medium degree of difficulty Time to prepare: 20 minutes

Garlic-based baked tomatoes

4 servings of ingredients:

600g beefsteak tomatoes

5 medium-sized garlic cloves 5 tbsp olive oil

4 thyme stalks pinch of salt pepper

Preparation:\sStep 1: Halve the tomatoes, remove the seeds. Roughly chop the thyme stalks & cut the garlic cloves into thin slices. Fry in a pan with 1 tablespoon of olive oil until golden. In a roasting pan, distribute the remaining oil,lay the tomatoes with the skin side down, sprinkle with roasted garlic and thyme.

Step 2: Put the dish in the oven for 20 minutes at 180 °C .

Total calories: 172 kcal Medium degree of difficulty Time to prepare: 30 minutes

Ingredients:

1 cauliflower

1 pinch of curry powder 50g grated Emmentaler 1 pinch of turmeric

1 tablespoon extra virgin olive oil

Preparation:\sStep 1: Preheat the oven to 180 °C and cut the cauliflower into fine florets. Shake florets with oil and curry powder in bowl.

Step 2: Prepare cauliflower on parchment paper in the oven for 20 minutes.

Total calories: 216 kcal Medium degree of difficulty Time to prepare: 30 minutes

Spinach gratin eggs and cheese

Ingredients:\s3 eggs

400g baby spinach 1 pinch of parsley 1 clove of garlic

15g parmesan cheese 1 tablespoon extra virgin olive oil Pinch of nutmeg

Preparation:

Step 1: hard boil eggs, collapse spinach in hot water and squeeze out. Chop the garlic, parsley, grate the parmesan. Drain the eggs, remove the shells and cut in half.

Step 2: Steam the garlic, then steam the spinach then season with pepper and nutmeg.

Step 3: Fill the baking dish with the spinach mixture, distribute the egg halves, sprinkle with parsley and parmesan, bake for 180 °C for 15 minutes.

Total calories: 261 kcal Medium degree of difficulty Time to prepare: 45 minutes

Croquette and cheese mix

Ingredients:

25g parmesan 25g Emmentaler egg\stbsp olive oil

½ cauliflower

30g breadcrumbs 1 bunch of chives

Preparation:\sStep 1: Preheat the oven to 180 °C degrees, boil the cauliflowerflorets in boiling water and make a porridge. Add the flour, parmesan, cheese, chives and egg and mix together.

Step 2: Form croquettes from the porridge and brush them with oil. Bake for 15 minutes.

Total calories: 276 kcal Medium degree of difficulty Time to prepare: 45 minutes

Kohlrabi lasagna

Ingredients:

400g kohlrabi 200g ground beef 100g grated cheese 50g cream cheese

50g crème fraîche (low fat) (low fat) Pinch of oregano

200g tomatoes salt and pepper

Preparation:\sStep 1: Cut the kohlrabi into slices and cook for around ten minutes. Sear the mince and season, add the tomatoes and cream cheese, stir, simmer for 5 minutes.

Step 2: Add a layer of minced sauce, a layer of kohlrabi, again minced sauce, then add crème fraîche. Add the sprinkled cheese.

Step 3: Bake everything for half an hour at 180 degrees.

Total calories: 672 kcal

Medium degree of difficulty

Time to prepare: 60 minutes

Veggie casserole with tofu

Ingredients:

300g butter vegetables

100g crème fraîche (low in fat) (low in fat) 300g tofu\s400g tomatoes

100g Emmentaler (litter) (litter)

Preparation:\sStep 1: Fill the baking dish with vegetables, crumble the tofu, add. Top with tomatoes. Mix the crème fraîche and tomato sauce, then mix with the cheese.

Total calories: 773 kcal Medium degree of difficulty Time to prepare: 45 minutes

Almond crunch with sweet potatoes

Ingredients:\s1kg sweet potatoes 150g goat cream cheese 1 clove of garlic\sspring onions

a tablespoon of soy sauce lemon juice, 2 tbsp 75g almonds

1 tbsp agave nectar Pepper, salt, chili powder

Preparation:\sStep 1: Cut the sweet potatoes into slices about 1 centimeter thick and cook them in salted water for about 15 minutes until they are nice and soft.

Step 2: Then chop the almonds and roast them in a pan.

Now cut the two spring onions into fine rolls.

Step 3: peel and finely chop the garlic. Mix together the soy sauce, agave syrup and lemon juice. Beat in the oil and season. If you like, season again with lemon and agave syrup.

Step 4: drain the sweet potatoes. Fry the potato slices in a little olive oil until golden brown. Mix all ingredients in a large salad bowl.

1 serving nutritional values:

Carbohydrates: 53g

Protein: 9g

Fat: 17g

Total calories: 410 kcal Medium degree of difficulty Time to prepare: 45 minutes

Tomato peppers pan

Ingredients:\s3 cloves of garlic\sglass of roasted red pepper 4 sprigs of thyme

small onions

400g cherry date tomatoes 1 small chilli pepper

2 tbsp extra virgin olive oil Tomato paste pepper sweetener pinch of salt

Preparation:\sStep 1: Drain the peppers, collect 150ml of juice. Peel the onion and cut it into thin strips. Then peel and squeeze the garlic cloves. Halve the chilli lengthways, remove the seeds and finely chop the pod. Finally, wash the thyme sprigs.

Step 2: Sauté onions, garlic, paprika, chilli in a pan. Stir in tomato paste, deglaze with paprika juice. Stir in tomatoes, thyme and sweetener. Let everything boil once and then simmer gently for another 5 minutes. Season to taste with salt and pepper.

Calories in total: 240 kcal Medium degree of difficulty Time to prepare: 20 minutes Salads

Chicken lettuce with mushrooms

ingredients

Lamb's lettuce

6 pieces of mushrooms 100g chicken\s20g parmesan cheese 3 tomatoes\steaspoon of olive oil

Preparation:\sStep 1: Cut the chicken into small pieces, then fry them.

Remove the stalk from the mushrooms, cut into slices, quarter the tomatoes.

Step 2: Mix all the ingredients together well and then sprinkle with parmesan cheese.

Total calories: 164 kcal Medium degree of difficulty Time to prepare: 20 minutes

Emmental salad on a Mediterranean basis

4 servings of ingredients:

zucchini

2 peppers (red) 400g Emmentaler a single garlic clove

1 teaspoon cayenne pepper

12 lemons

3 stalks of chives

Sea salt, pepper, olive oil Preparation: Step 1: Cut the zucchini in half lengthways and cut halfway into slices. Halve and core the peppers and remove the white inner walls. Finely chop the garlic and cut the bell pepper into fine strips. Fry the zucchini and peppers in a pan for 2-3 minutes until they are lightly browned. Stir in the garlic and season the vegetables.

Step 2: Halve the lemon and squeeze out the juice, cut the chives into rolls. Dice the cheese, mix with the vegetables, lemon juice and chives.

Total calories: 480 kcal Medium degree of difficulty Time to prepare: 15 minutes

Watermelon Cherry Salad

Ingredients for a four-person meal:

500g watermelon\s0.5 pomegranate 250g cherries

half an organic orange 250g raspberries

2 teaspoons of lime juice

Preparation:\sStep 1: Cut out the flesh of the watermelon and dice.

Halve the cherries. Loosen the pomegranate seeds from the pomegranate and remove the white pieces of skin. Sieve the kernels off using a fine sieve.

Step 2: Finely rub the peel of the orange and then squeeze out the juice. Finally, mix all the ingredients together to make a fruit salad.

Total calories: 130 kcal Medium degree of difficulty Time to prepare: 20 minutes

Potato and chickpea salad

Ingredients:\s1 kg of spring potatoes Chickpeas - fresh or canned a single onion

1 pinch of salt

1 organic lemon pepper

100g stone-free black olives 400g cherry date tomatoes 4 parsley stalks

a single garlic clove

1-2 teaspoons of liquid honey mustard

4 tbsp extra virgin olive oil

Ingredients:\sStep 1: Wash the spring potatoes well and cook them in boiling salted water for about 20 minutes. Then drain the chickpeas well and cut the tomatoes in half in half. Also peel the onion, cut it in half and cut each half into fine strips. Let the olives drain well and then chop them very finely. If you want, you can leave the olives whole.

Step 2: Now pour the potatoes and cut them into larger pieces. Then put these salad ingredients in a large bowl.

Step 3: Rinse the organic lemon with hot, pat it dry and then rub the peel off. Then cut the lemon in half and finally squeeze out the juice. Pluck the parsley leaves from the stems and finely chop the leaves. Finally, peel the garlic and finely chop it too. Mix everything in a bowl and stir in the honey and mustard. Gradually add the olive oil and season everything with pepper and a pinch of salt.

Step 4: Mix the salad with this dressing and serve it with the potatoes and chickpeas.

Total calories: 360 kcal Medium degree of difficulty Time to prepare: 40 minutes

Spicy BBQ salad boats

Ingredients:

two garlic cloves

8 cherry date tomatoes two garlic cloves 300g minced beef 150g basmati rice olive oil

2 lettuce hearts sea-salt Cayenne pepper Smoked peppers BBQ sauce

Preparation:\sStep 1: Cook the rice, dice the garlic cloves & onion. Now cut the tomatoes in half & put everything in a large bowl.

Step 2: Sear the ground beef, season, add the onions and tomatoes to the pan for about 5 minutes.

Step 3: Wash lettuce leaves, mix with rice and mince mixture, add BBQ sauce.

Medium degree of difficulty Time to prepare: 40 minutes

Thai style crab meat salad

Ingredients for 4 servings:\speppers\spapayas (small to medium-sized) (small to medium-sized) 350g meat from crab

1 shallot chili

1 ginger

1.5 tbsp sugar coriander

3 tbsp Thai meat sauce 2 tbsp rice vinegar

Preparation:\sStep 1: First quarter the peppers and cut them into small cubes. Finely chop the shallot, peel the papaya, also cut into 5mm cubes. Peel the ginger and cut it as finely as possible. Halve the chilli pepper, chop finely.

Step 2: Mix the finely chopped ginger with 2 tablespoons of water, the Thai meat sauce, the rice vinegar, the sugar and a pinch of salt. Make sure that the sugar and also the salt dissolve completely. Then mix all the ingredients you have prepared together in a kitchen bowl.

Step 3: Pluck the coriander leaves, wash and finely chop them.

Step 4: Cut the remaining papayas in half and remove the seeds. Line the papaya halves with coriander and fill in the lettuce.

Total calories: 146 kcal Medium degree of difficulty Time to prepare: 20 minutes

Bean salad with tuna meatballs

Ingredients:\s150g green beans 1 shallot\s120g tuna (in its own juice) (in its own juice) 1 spring onion

2 teaspoons ajvar

a single egg

1 tbsp capers

3 tbsp oatmeal

½ bunch of parsley\stbsp apple cider vinegar 1 teaspoon agave syrup\stbsp rapeseed oil Salt, mill pepper

Preparation:

Step 1: Halve the beans, cook until al dente, finely chop the shallot and add to the beans. Finely chop the spring onion, mix the tuna with the onion, ajvar, capers, oat flakes, egg, capers, salt and pepper. Shape the mixture into balls with your hands, fry for 4 minutes. Step 2: Roughly chop the parsley, mix the oil, vinegar, agave syrup with beans and parsley. Mix the meatballs with the salad.

Total calories: 430 kcal Medium degree of difficulty Time to prepare: 20 minutes

Chapter 6

Bean salad on ginger and wasabi

Ingredients:\s30g radicchio 1 small chicory\s150g thick beans

small celery stalks 3 parsley stalks

peppermint stalks

100g rocket or lamb's lettuce 1 small piece of ginger\stablespoon of juice from one lime 2 teaspoons of wasabi paste

tbsp sesame oil 3 tbsp soy sauce

1 tbsp agave nectar

Preparation:\sStep 1: First, blanch the beans in boiling salted water for about 8 minutes. Pluck the radicchio and chicory and cut into small pieces. Now cut the celery stalks into fine slices. Now pluck the herbs from the stems, wash them and chop them as finely as possible. Drain the beans, rinse, drain and peel them off the skin.

Step 2: Cut the unpeeled ginger into pieces, press in the garlic press until the juice comes out. Whisk lime juice, wasabi paste, soy sauce, oil, agave syrup and 1 tbsp water.

Step 3: Mix the lettuce, broad beans, and celery in the salad bowl. Fold in the dressing.

Total calories: 230 kcal Medium degree of difficulty Time to prepare: 40 minutes

White cabbage coconut curry

Ingredients:

a single garlic clove 1 turkey schnitzel

½ small chilli pepper\s¾ soybean oil 200g carrots\s500g white cabbage

1 bunch of spring onions 50ml coconut milk

125g chunky tomatoes 1 stalk of coriander

1 tbsp roasted peanut kernel Salt, pepper and curry powder

Preparation:\sStep 1: cut the garlic clove into thin slices. Halve, core and then chop the chilli pepper. Halve turkey escalope,mix with half of the garlic slices and chilli pepper as well as 1 teaspoon of oil. Cut the cabbage into strips, cut the peeled carrots into sticks, cut the spring onions into pieces.

Step 2: Sauté vegetables in oil, season and add coconut milk and garlic slices. Cover and let everything simmer for about a quarter of an hour. Stir in tomatoes and let simmer for another 15 minutes.

Step 3: Fry the turkey schnitzel, roughly chop the peanuts.

Wash the coriander, let the leaves dry well, and then pluck the leaves. Arrange everything together. Total calories: 462 kcal Medium degree of difficulty Time to prepare: 40 minutes

Cashew salad with sweet potatoes

4 servings of ingredients:

600g sweet potatoes 60g cashew nuts

1 bunch of coriander\s½ bunch of basil 10g mint

1 onion, red 15g ginger root

3 tsp (30g) (30g) coconut blossom sugar 6 tbsp lime juice

Cayenne pepper, salt 2 tbsp extra virgin olive oil

1 tblsp sesame seed oil

Preparation:\sStep 1: Cut the sweet potatoes into thin slices and cook them in salted water until they are soft. Roast the cashew nuts without oil, finely chop the coriander, mint and basil leaves. Now peel the ginger and the onion and chop it finely.

Step 2: Drain the sweet potatoes, stir in the ginger, lime juice, sugar, cayenne pepper, salt, olive oil and sesame oil to form a vinaigrette.

Step 3: Mix the herbs, sweet potato slices, cashew nuts and onions and stir in the vinaigrette.

Calories in total: 355 kcal Medium degree of difficulty Time to prepare: 40 minutes Desserts

Vanilla ice cream with a creamy texture

ingredients

4 beaten egg whites 120ml distilled water

Vanilla extract or vanilla flavor may be used instead of fresh vanilla pulp. 2 tablespoons sugar

Step 1: In a mixing bowl, combine the egg powder, water, and beat with a mixer for approximately 10 minutes. Add the vanilla pulp and sugar while mixing.

Step 2: Freeze the ingredients for around 60 minutes.

Step 3: Re-whip the semi-frozen mixture briefly before dividing it into cups or glasses (makes 2 servings).

Calories in total: 100 kcal Medium degree of difficulty Time to prepare: 90 minutes

Noodles fried in applesauce

ingredients

Vanilla-flavored protein powder, 80 g 2 beaten egg whites

two eggs

2 delicious apples 1 tablespoon sugar

1 cinnamon sachet

12 teaspoon extract de vanille

Step 1: Peel, core, and quarter the apples, then simmer until tender in a small pot with 1cm of water. Puree till smooth, seasoning with a bit of cinnamon. Step 2: Combine all other ingredients in a mixing bowl for 2 minutes, then spread thinly on a baking sheet lined with parchment paper. Bake for a quarter of an hour at 180°C.

Step 3: Slice the chilled pond into thin strips and brown in a skillet with 1 teaspoon coconut oil for a few minutes. Serve with applesauce on the side.

Calories in total: 335 kcal Medium degree of difficulty Time to prepare: 60 minutes Snacks with less than 100 calories

Smoothie with berries

ingredients

100g currants 200ml water 100 grams of raspberries

As required, agave syrup

Step 1: Wash the berries well and blend them with the water to form a fine smoothie. Add water and agave syrup as needed.

Calories in total: 76 kcal Level of difficulty: easy Time to prepare: 5 minutes

stuffed peppers with couscous

ingredients

1 orange pepper, tiny

1 yellow tiny bell pepper 1 red tiny bell pepper 100g couscous (cooked)

1 onion (spring) 100 grams of zucchini 4 different types of mushrooms

3 coriander stalks

1 lemon, freshly squeezed nutmeg, salt, and pepper

Step 1: Dice the mushrooms, spring onions, zucchini, and two different colored pepper halves into tiny cubes.

Step 2: Cook the couscous and cut the coriander finely.

Combine all of the ingredients in a large mixing bowl and season with lemon juice to taste. Fill the pepper halves halfway with the filling.

Step 3: Serve cold as a snack or bake for 20 minutes at 180°C in the oven.

Calories in total: 75 kcal Medium degree of difficulty Time to prepare: 30 minutes

Yogurt-dipped vegetable sticks

ingredients

60 g fat-free natural yogurt Carrots, 100g

celery sticks (100g) herbs, salt, and pepper

Step 1: Wash and peel all of the veggies before cutting them into small strips. Step 2: Season the yogurt with salt and pepper and serve as a dip.

Calories in total: 97 kcal Level of difficulty: easy Time to prepare: 10 minutes

Spicy chicken jelly

Ingredients for a four-person meal:

6 gelatin sheets (white) 100 milliliters white wine (dry)

75 mL tomato juice + 75 mL chicken broth 1 leaf of bay

5 black peppercorns

250g pieces of chicken breast 5 flat leaf parsley green salad stems

red pepper (200g)

1 teaspoon powdered paprika mustard seeds (1 teaspoon) red wine vinegar, 2 tbsp

Step 1: Soak the gelatine in cold water, slice the shallots into rings, and bring the white wine, tomato juice, paprika powder, broth, mustard seeds, bay leaf, and peppercorns to a boil. Squeeze the gelatine out and dissolve it in boiling water, then add the vinegar and soak for approximately 25 minutes.

Step 2: Quarter and core the peppers, then lay them on a baking sheet skin side up. The peppers should be roasted until the skin becomes black. The bell peppers should then be placed in a bowl and covered for approximately a quarter of an hour. The peppers should then be peeled and sliced into 12 cm strips.

Step 3: Make wider strips out of the chicken breast fillet. Chop the parsley and combine it with the paprika strips, parsley, and cold cuts in a mixing bowl. Add some spice to your life. Divide the mixture into four molds, then pour the chilled stock into the molds and refrigerate for six minutes.

Step 4: Invert the molds in hot water and drape with lettuce.

Calories in total: 99kcal Medium degree of difficulty Time to prepare: 50 minutes

Hummus made with pumpkin

12 servings of ingredients:

220g pumpkin from Hokkaido chickpeas, 220g

4 tablespoons tahini

3 tbsp extra virgin olive oil juice of a lemon

3 stalks coriander

2 tablespoons caraway seeds 1 teaspoon turmeric (salt)

pumpkin seeds, 2 tbsp flakes of chilli

Step 1: Halve the Hokkaido pumpkin, remove the seeds, and chop the pulp into tiny pieces. Cook for 10 minutes in boiling water. In a blender, combine the chickpeas, oil, tahini, lemon juice, cumin, salt, and turmeric, as well as 50ml water.

Step 2: Blend in the pumpkin as well, until it is finely puréed. Coriander should be chopped. In a bowl, combine the hummus, pumpkin seeds, chili flakes, and coriander.

Calories in total: 77kcal Medium degree of difficulty Time to prepare: 30 minutes

Lucky rolls in the Vietnamese style

4 servings of ingredients:

100g carrots 16 pages rice paper

25 grams of glass noodles

150 g fillet de poulet de poulet de poulet de poulet de poulet (cooked) lettuce leaves (eight)

Cucumber, 100g

6 stalks coriander

1 tblsp sesame seed oil

Step 1: Soak the rice paper for 1 minute in warm water. In a dish, pour boiling water over glass noodles and let aside to cook. Peel the cucumber and carrots and cut them lengthwise into extremely fine strips, then cut the chicken breast fillet into very small slices.

Step 2: Cut the lettuce into finger-width strips by removing the core ribs. Wash and pluck the coriander leaves. Glass noodles should be strained and cut into shorter pieces using kitchen scissors. In a mixing bowl, combine the veggies, meat, pasta, and seasonings.

Step 3: Place the mixture in the center of the rice paper and gently wrap it up. Cut the rolls lengthwise diagonally.

Calories in total: 98 kcal Medium degree of difficulty Time to prepare: 30 minutesCalories in total: 355 kcal Medium degree of difficulty Time to prepare: 40 minutes Desserts

Vanilla ice cream with a creamy texture

ingredients

4 beaten egg whites 120ml distilled water

Vanilla extract or vanilla flavor may be used instead of fresh vanilla pulp. 2 tablespoons sugar

Step 1: In a mixing bowl, combine the egg powder, water, and beat with a mixer for approximately 10 minutes. Add the vanilla pulp and sugar while mixing.

Step 2: Freeze the ingredients for around 60 minutes.

Step 3: Re-whip the semi-frozen mixture briefly before dividing it into cups or glasses (makes 2 servings).

Calories in total: 100 kcal Medium degree of difficulty Time to prepare: 90 minutes

Noodles fried in applesauce

ingredients

Vanilla-flavored protein powder, 80 g 2 beaten egg whites

two eggs

2 delicious apples 1 tablespoon sugar

1 cinnamon sachet

12 teaspoon extract de vanille

Step 1: Peel, core, and quarter the apples, then simmer until tender in a small pot with 1cm of water. Puree till smooth, seasoning with a bit of cinnamon. Step 2: Combine all other ingredients in a mixing bowl for 2 minutes, then spread thinly on a baking sheet lined with parchment paper. Bake for a quarter of an hour at 180°C.

Step 3: Slice the chilled pond into thin strips and brown in a skillet with 1 teaspoon coconut oil for a few minutes. Serve with applesauce on the side.

Calories in total: 335 kcal Medium degree of difficulty Time to prepare: 60 minutes Snacks with less than 100 calories

Smoothie with berries

ingredients

100g currants 200ml water 100 grams of raspberries

As required, agave syrup

Step 1: Wash the berries well and blend them with the water to form a fine smoothie. Add water and agave syrup as needed.

Calories in total: 76 kcal Level of difficulty: easy Time to prepare: 5 minutes

stuffed peppers with couscous

ingredients

1 orange pepper, tiny

1 yellow tiny bell pepper 1 red tiny bell pepper 100g couscous (cooked)

1 onion (spring) 100 grams of zucchini 4 different types of mushrooms

3 coriander stalks

1 lemon, freshly squeezed nutmeg, salt, and pepper

Step 1: Dice the mushrooms, spring onions, zucchini, and two different colored pepper halves into tiny cubes.

Step 2: Cook the couscous and cut the coriander finely.

Combine all of the ingredients in a large mixing bowl and season with lemon juice to taste. Fill the pepper halves halfway with the filling.

Step 3: Serve cold as a snack or bake for 20 minutes at 180°C in the oven.

Calories in total: 75 kcal Medium degree of difficulty Time to prepare: 30 minutes

Yogurt-dipped vegetable sticks

ingredients

60 g fat-free natural yogurt Carrots, 100g

celery sticks (100g) herbs, salt, and pepper

Step 1: Wash and peel all of the veggies before cutting them into small strips. Step 2: Season the yogurt with salt and pepper and serve as a dip.

Calories in total: 97 kcal Level of difficulty: easy Time to prepare: 10 minutes

Spicy chicken jelly

Ingredients for a four-person meal:

6 gelatin sheets (white) 100 milliliters white wine (dry)

75 mL tomato juice + 75 mL chicken broth 1 leaf of bay

5 black peppercorns

250g pieces of chicken breast 5 flat leaf parsley green salad stems

red pepper (200g)

1 teaspoon powdered paprika mustard seeds (1 teaspoon) red wine vinegar, 2 tbsp

Step 1: Soak the gelatine in cold water, slice the shallots into rings, and bring the white wine, tomato juice, paprika powder, broth, mustard seeds, bay leaf, and peppercorns to a boil. Squeeze the gelatine out and dissolve it in boiling water, then add the vinegar and soak for approximately 25 minutes.

Step 2: Quarter and core the peppers, then lay them on a baking sheet skin side up. The peppers should be roasted until the skin becomes black. The bell peppers should then be placed in a bowl and covered for approximately a quarter of an hour. The peppers should then be peeled and sliced into 12 cm strips.

Step 3: Make wider strips out of the chicken breast fillet. Chop the parsley and combine it with the paprika strips, parsley, and cold cuts in a mixing bowl. Add some spice to your life. Divide the mixture into four molds, then pour the chilled stock into the molds and refrigerate for six minutes.

Step 4: Invert the molds in hot water and drape with lettuce.

Calories in total: 99kcal Medium degree of difficulty Time to prepare: 50 minutes

Hummus made with pumpkin

12 servings of ingredients:

220g pumpkin from Hokkaido chickpeas, 220g

4 tablespoons tahini

3 tbsp extra virgin olive oil juice of a lemon

3 stalks coriander

2 tablespoons caraway seeds 1 teaspoon turmeric (salt)

pumpkin seeds, 2 tbsp flakes of chilli

Step 1: Halve the Hokkaido pumpkin, remove the seeds, and chop the pulp into tiny pieces. Cook for 10 minutes in boiling water. In a blender, combine the chickpeas, oil, tahini, lemon juice, cumin, salt, and turmeric, as well as 50ml water.

Step 2: Blend in the pumpkin as well, until it is finely puréed. Coriander should be chopped. In a bowl, combine the hummus, pumpkin seeds, chili flakes, and coriander.

Calories in total: 77kcal Medium degree of difficulty Time to prepare: 30 minutes

Lucky rolls in the Vietnamese style

4 servings of ingredients:

100g carrots 16 pages rice paper

25 grams of glass noodles

150 g fillet de poulet de poulet de poulet de poulet de poulet (cooked) lettuce leaves (eight)

Cucumber, 100g

6 stalks coriander

1 tblsp sesame seed oil

Step 1: Soak the rice paper for 1 minute in warm water. In a dish, pour boiling water over glass noodles and let aside to cook. Peel the cucumber and carrots and cut them lengthwise into extremely fine strips, then cut the chicken breast fillet into very small slices.

Step 2: Cut the lettuce into finger-width strips by removing the core ribs. Wash and pluck the coriander leaves. Glass noodles should be strained and cut into shorter pieces using kitchen scissors. In a mixing bowl, combine the veggies, meat, pasta, and seasonings.

Step 3: Place the mixture in the center of the rice paper and gently wrap it up. Cut the rolls lengthwise diagonally.

Calories in total: 98 kcal Medium degree of difficulty Time to prepare: 30 minutes